Managing Editor
Mara Ellen Guckian

Editor in Chief
Karen J. Goldfluss, M.S. Ed.

Creative Director
Sarah M. Fornier

Illustrator
Kelly McMahon

Cover Artist
Diem Pascarella

Art Coordinator
Renée Mc Elwee

Imaging
Craig Gunnell
James Edward Grace

Publisher
Mary D. Smith, M.S. Ed.

Author
Mara Ellen Guckian

Teacher Created Resources
12621 Western Avenue
Garden Grove, CA 92841
www.teachercreated.com
ISBN: 978-1-4206-8003-4

© 2016 Teacher Created Resources
Made in U.S.A.

Table of Contents

Introduction

Welcome to a workbook filled with fun for young learners! Each page in this book is designed to guide parent and child in exploring and developing the skills he or she will use in school. The topics, or subject areas, are arranged as follows:

- **Line Practice**—printing straight, diagonal, curved, and wiggly lines
- **The Alphabet**—recognizing letters and letter sounds; printing uppercase and lowercase letters
- **Thinking Skills**—learning to look at things in different ways—to consider options; to analyze, to infer, to interpret data, and to solve problems of all kinds
- **Numbers (1–10)**—numbers; number sense; sequencing; size; shapes; more, less, and equal
- **Science and Nature** —noticing animals and their habitats; observing growing things; developing an awareness of the human body and the five senses; comparing the seasons
- **Social Studies**—focusing on family and homes, neighborhoods; community helpers, workers, work vehicles; caring for our planet

How to Use This Book

New skills and concepts are described on the "Parent Information" page at the beginning of each section. Use these guidelines to guide children toward a better understanding of each activity.

The directions at the top of each activity page provide helpful information. They can be read to a child to help him or her practice listening skills and used as a guide to help you work together.

- Practice listening and speaking skills and take turns discussing the pictures and the tasks.
- Use complete sentences and work on using descriptive language.
- Remember to start at the top of each page or line. Work down, and from left to right. This will provide practice reading from left to right.
- Use the gray tracing lines provided to help your child practice drawing lines and later printing letters and numbers.
- Your child might be asked to circle an item, to color an object, or to count in groups. Work with your child to follow these directions accurately.
- Identify colors whenever possible and use position words correctly (*on, off, in,* etc.).

The *Look Around!* suggestions at the bottom of each page will reinforce the lesson while extending it to a higher level by asking questions to make children think about what they are learning. Some suggestions can be done inside, and others are best suited for outside activities—perhaps while walking or exploring at a park or playground. For instance, if you are working on the number 3, you might focus on finding the number 3 on street addresses or license plates, or you might arrange things in 3s—like blocks or apples. In this way, the topic or concept will relate more to your child's everyday life.

Most of all, have fun with your child! Neither you nor your child should feel stressed if an activity seems too difficult at the time. Remember that children learn in different ways and at different times. It's okay to help your child trace, color, or identify an object with a little coaxing. The time you spend together with these activities is precious, and you will be surprised at how much your child has actually learned by the time you complete them.

Developamental Skills and Concepts

The activities in this book will enable students to build competence in the following areas:

Printing
- holding a pencil and paper correctly
- making straight, diagonal, and curved lines
- writing from left to right
- writing from top to bottom

The Alphabet
- recognizing and naming letters (Aa–Zz)
- writing the correct form of each letter
- understanding that letters make sounds
- matching beginning sounds to objects
- observing print in writing
- using capital letters for names
- repeating words and sounds
- printing names

Thinking Skills/Speaking and Listening
- observing closely
- listening attentively to directions
- speaking in complete sentences
- comparing and contrasting items and ideas
- considering and discussing different options, approaches, or responses
- using positional words to describe relationships among objects

Numbers and Numeracy
- identifying numbers 1–10
- making one-to-one correspondences (understanding "how many")
- identifying shapes—circle, triangle, square, rectangle, oval, rhombus
- recognizing and comparing sizes—large, small, short, tall, etc.
- determining more, less, or equal

Science
- comparing animals and their habitats
- observing plants and other living things
- discussing the human body—how it works, and what is needed to keep it healthy
- using the senses to explore and observe materials
- making comparisons among objects; identifying similarities and differences
- understanding how living things function, adapt, and change
- naming major body parts and their functions
- describing basic needs of living things, such as air and water
- differentiating between seasons and observing changes in nature

Social Studies
- understanding the idea of family
- comparing different types of homes
- exploring one's neighborhood
- observing community helpers and other workers
- understanding the need to care for Earth through conservation and recycling

How to Hold a Pencil

Better Posture

Poor Posture

Good posture is important.

1. Sit with your feet flat on the floor.

2. Sit back in the chair, and don't slouch.

3. Lean slightly forward.

4. Try to keep your elbows off the table.

Pencil position is important.

1. Hold the pencil between the thumb and first two fingers (index and middle).

2. The length of the pencil should rest near the large knuckle of the index finger.

3. At the pointed end, the index finger rests on the top of the pencil, and the pencil rests on top of the middle finger.

4. Maintain an easy grip on the pencil—not too loose, not too tight!

5. Hold the pencil close to the pointed end, not the eraser end.

6. Make a game of "Grasp and Release." Keep picking up and dropping a pencil using the correct grip. Play until it is second nature to grab the pencil correctly.

Helpful Hints

1. A certain level of muscle development is required in one's fingers to hold a pencil correctly and to guide it to form letters correctly. To help young writers, be sure to provide opportunities to strengthen hand and finger muscles. Offer opportunities to work with clay, dough, small clamp-together block sets (like Legos®), and other activities where hands work to manipulate items.

2. Some children benefit from adaptations when learning to write. Try one or more of the following ideas to help your child learn the proper pencil grip.

   • Use a rubber or plastic pencil grip. These can be purchased in teacher and office supply stores.

   • Try using a short pencil, like a golf-scoring pencil. This shorter pencil will encourage the holder to hold it closer to the pointed end.

Line Practice

Being able to write (print) fluently is a skill—one all children need to learn. Writing enables them to express themselves on paper. Writing legibly enables their "readers" to understand their thoughts. This becomes particularly important during school and later in life.

Using a pencil or crayon effectively is very important when learning to print letters. To do this, children need to develop muscle strength in their hands, wrists, and fingers. There are many ways to help young "writers" improve their fine motor skills and dexterity, including the following:

- Work with clay or knead dough.
- Grip and squeeze small balls.
- Build with interlocking blocks such as Unifix® Cubes or Legos®.
- Pick things up (buttons, cotton balls, etc.) using tongs or tweezers.
- Open and close things.
- Get dressed—work with buttons, zippers, Velcro®, and shoelaces.

Getting Started

In this section, encourage your child to trace the gray lines first, using his or her index finger (pointer finger). Start at the top of each letter and move in a downward motion. Encourage your child to write from left to right when possible. Start good habits early!

Help your child sit correctly and hold the writing implement properly. (See page 5.) Then, have him or her use a pencil or crayon to trace the gray lines to complete each page. Start at the arrow and try to continue to the end of each line without lifting up the pencil. Discuss each type of line and how it is drawn.

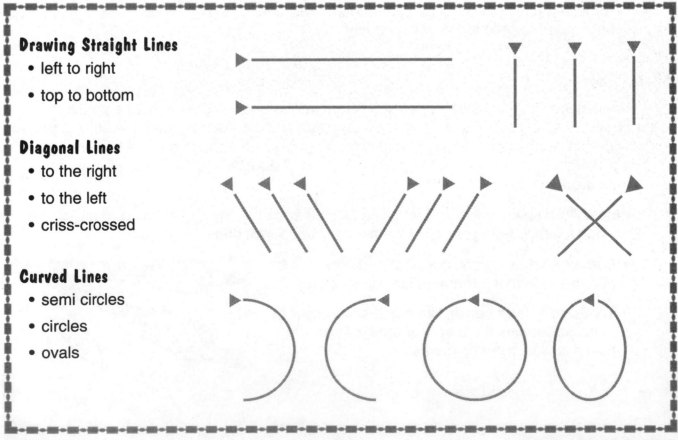

Drawing Straight Lines
- left to right
- top to bottom

Diagonal Lines
- to the right
- to the left
- criss-crossed

Curved Lines
- semi circles
- circles
- ovals

Straight Lines

Directions: Trace the straight, gray lines with your finger before using a pencil. Notice that some lines go across horizontally and others are vertical lines that go from top to bottom.

Start at the arrow for each straight line. Try to continue to the end of each line without lifting up the pencil.

This activity can be done over and over again using different colors, creating rainbow lines.

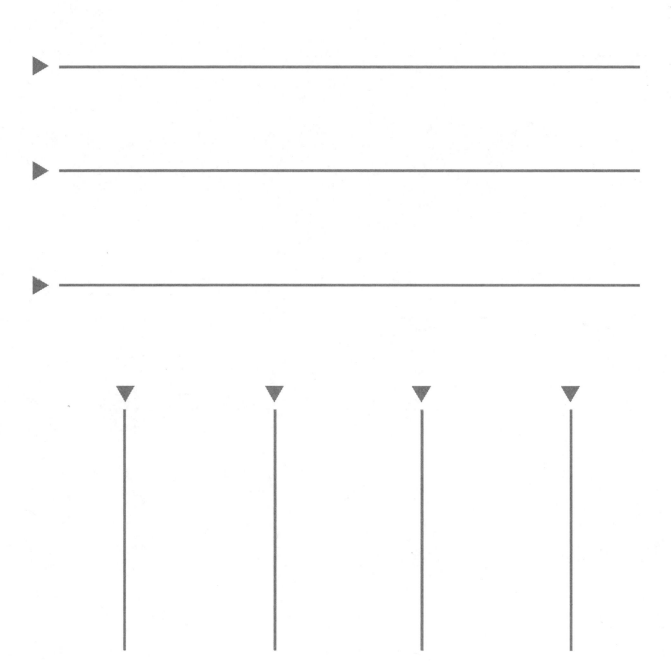

Look Around! Can you find some straight lines? (*edges of tables or counters, sidewalks, windows*) Which direction are the lines going?

Diagonal Lines

Directions: Trace the gray diagonal lines with your finger before using a pencil. Notice that each line starts at the top and moves downward. Some go to the right and some go to the left.

Start at the arrow for each line. Try to continue to the end of each line without lifting up the pencil.

This activity can be done over and over again using different colors, creating rainbow lines.

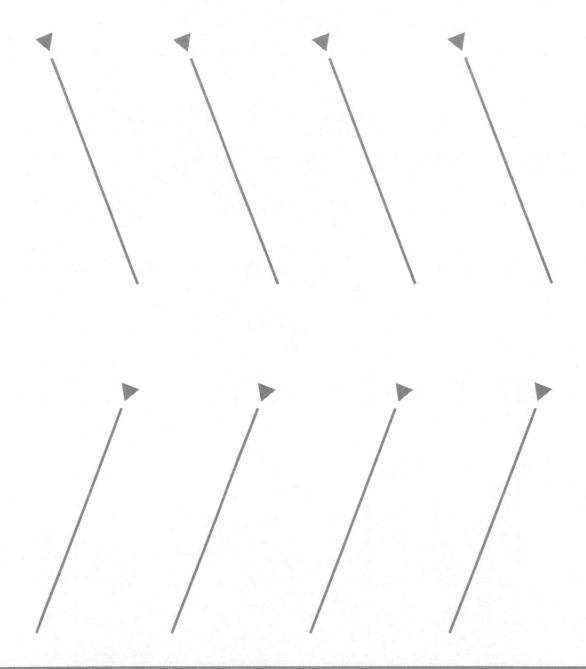

Look Around! Can you find some diagonal lines? (*roofs, swing sets, triangular-shaped signs*)

Crisscrossed Lines

Directions: Trace the gray diagonal lines with your finger before using a pencil. Notice that each line starts at the top and moves downward. Some go to the right and some go to the left. They cross in the middle.

Start at the arrow for each line. Try to continue to the end of each line without lifting up the pencil.

This activity can be done over and over again using different colors, creating rainbow lines.

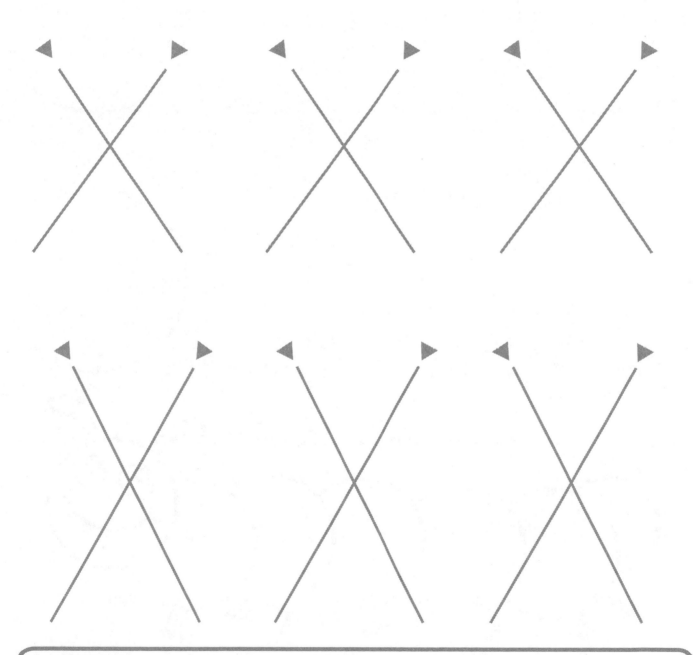

Look Around! Can you find some diagonal lines that cross? (*lattice fences, signs with X, tiles in the floor or bathroom, etc.*)

Curve to the Left!

Directions: Trace the gray curved lines with your finger before using a pencil. Notice that each line starts at the top and moves around to the left and down. Start at the arrow for each line. Try to continue to the end of each line without lifting up the pencil.

Connecting your curves can make a caterpillar! Color the caterpillar green.

Look Around! Can you find some curved lines in your house?

Curve to the Right!

Directions: Trace the gray curved lines with your finger before using a pencil. Notice that each line starts at the top and moves around to the right and down.

Start at the arrow for each line. Try to continue to the end of each line without lifting up the pencil.

This activity can be done over and over again using different colors, creating rainbow lines.

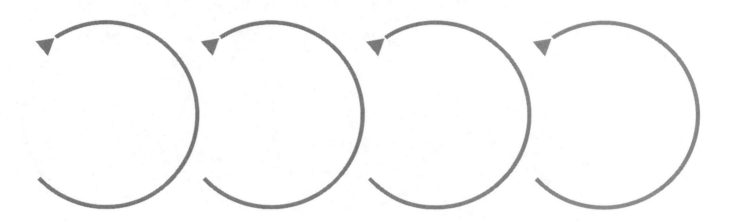

Connecting your curves can make a string of beads! Color the beads different colors.

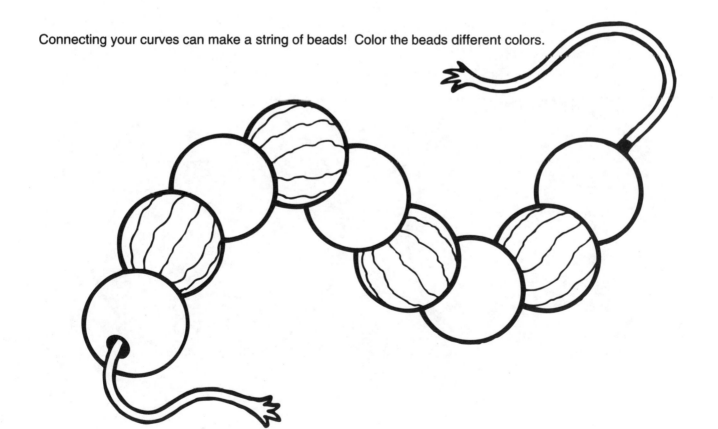

Look Around! Can you find some curved lines outside? (*rolling hills, half moon, etc.*)

Curve All Around

Directions: Trace the gray curved lines with your finger before using a pencil. What is different about these curved lines? Start at the arrow, move toward the left, and complete the curve.

Try to continue to the end of each circle of without lifting up the pencil. What did you make?

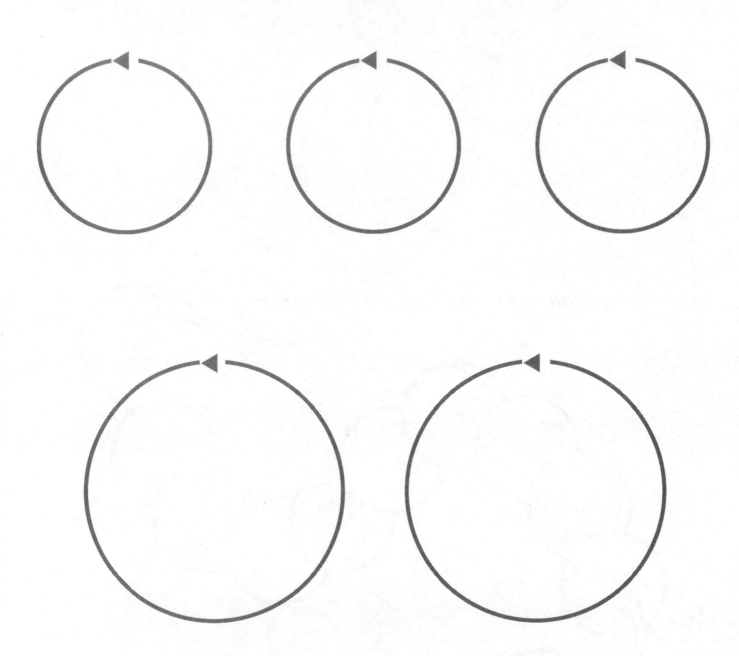

Look Around! Draw a snowman by placing one circle on top of another circle. Decorate it and add a face. Can you find some circles? (*moon, headlights, etc.*)

Circles in Circles

Directions: Use a pencil to trace over the gray curved lines. Start with the arrow on the outside circle, curve around to the left and finish back at the arrow. Do the same for each circle, working in to the center. How many circles did you make?

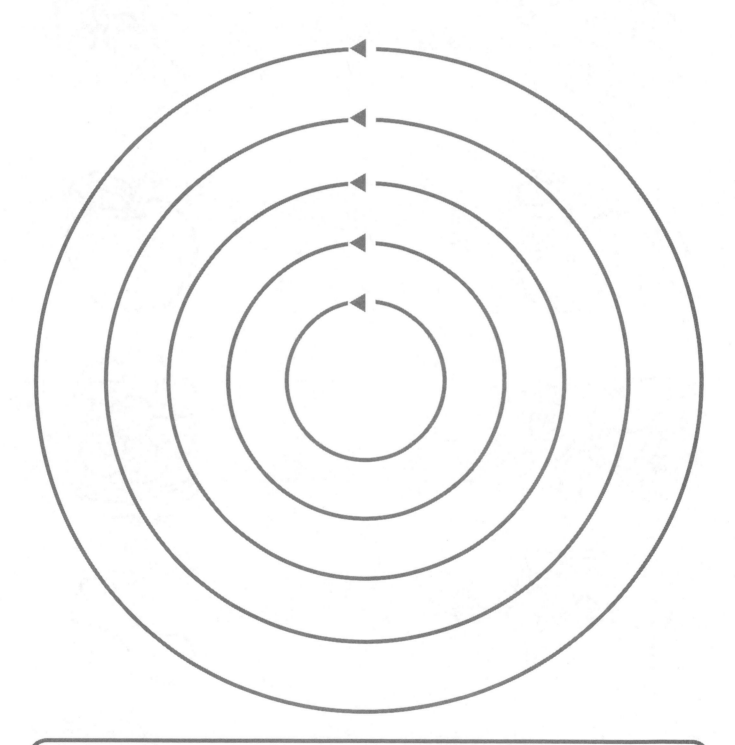

Look Around! Can you find some circles inside circles? (*a target, stacking bowls, etc.*)

Left to Right

Directions: Trace the gray dashed lines with your finger. Draw lines from left to right to match each animal to one of its favorite things.

Wiggly Lines

Directions: Trace the gray dashed lines with your finger. Move from left to right. Then draw the lines to connect each pair of shoes.

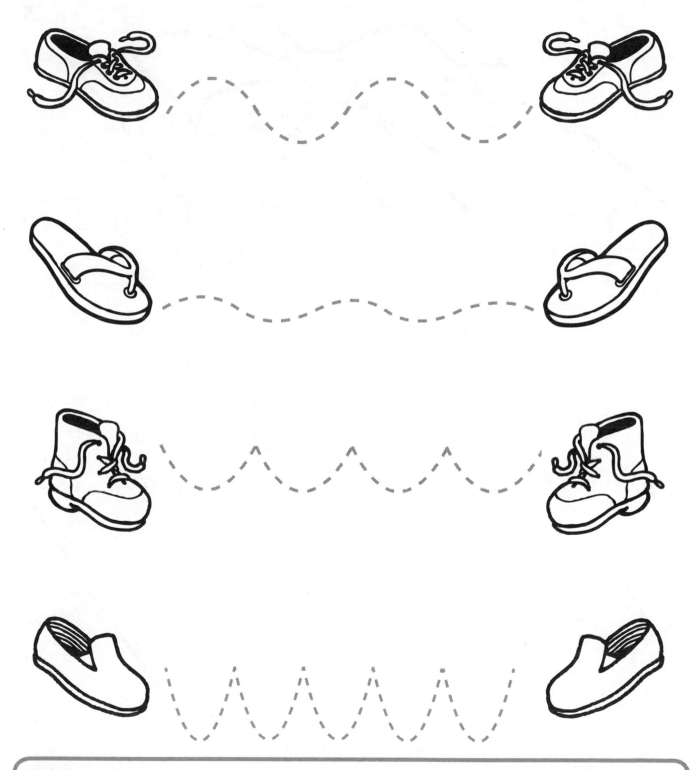

Look Around! Can you find a pattern with wiggly lines? Draw some wiggly lines using crayons, markers, or chalk.

Finish the Present

Directions: Use a pencil to draw the straight dashed lines to complete the picture. Color the finished picture.

Look Around! Find something that has straight lines and no curves! A skyscraper? A table? Floor tiles?

Finish the House

Directions: Use a pencil to trace the diagonal dashed lines to complete the picture of the house. Color the finished picture.

Look Around! Look for diagonal lines in your house or in your neighborhood. Walk in a diagonal line on the sidewalk. Zigzag back and forth.

Finish the Watermelon

Directions: Use a pencil to trace the curved dashed lines to finish the watermelon and the slice. Color the finished picture.

Look Around! Find some curves. Next time you are in a car, notice the streets. Do they have curvy or straight lines? Look at the play structures at the park. Do they have curved or straight lines?

#8003 1-2-3 Learn   18   ©Teacher Created Resources

Find Their Homes

Directions: Look at the animals in the first column and the animal homes in the second column. Draw a line from each animal to its home.

Look Around! Can you find some animal homes in your home or outside? (*doghouse, bird's nest, beehive, bunny hutch, gopher holes, etc.*)

The Alphabet

Most children are excited to learn to print—especially their own names! For most, learning the "shapes" of the letters comes first. Some children learn to write the letters of the alphabet in order, while others benefit from learning all the straight-line letters first and then the curved-line letters. The letters in this section are presented alphabetically but can be done in any order to suit your child's needs or interests.

Getting Started

In this section, your child will be using the skills practiced in the previous unit and noticing how different types of lines are used to form each uppercase and lowercase letter. Encourage your child to first trace the letters and then to practice writing them in the spaces provided. This will help him or her understand which direction each letter goes. It is not unusual for children just learning to write to "draw" some letters upside down or backwards. Initially, the letters are shapes. With practice, children learn that each letter should be drawn in a specific manner and that each letter has a specific sound or sounds attributed to it.

There are three pictures on each alphabet letter page that begin with the featured letter. Use these pictures to highlight the primary sound attributed to the letter. Explain that some letters, especially the vowels (*a, e, i, o, u,* and sometimes *y*) can make a variety of sounds depending on the letters around them. (*Note:* The exception is the letter *X* in which the pictures start or end in the letter.)

Expand this beginning-sounds discussion to notice other things in the house or the neighborhood that start with the same beginning sound. Slowly, your child will begin to understand that each letter makes one or more sounds and that when combined, these letters/sounds form words.

Skills to Practice

- Hold the pencil or crayon and the paper correctly.
- Write from left to right.
- Write from top to bottom.
- Recognize and name letters.
- Understand that letters make sounds.
- Write the correct form of each uppercase and lowercase letter.
- Print his/her own name legibly.

Aa

Directions: Look at the uppercase letter **A** and the lowercase letter **a**. Talk about the different lines used to make each one. Trace the letters and then print each one. Look at the pictures of things that start with the letter **A**. Listen to the different sounds the letter **A** makes at the beginning of each item pictured.

Look Around! Can you find other things that start with the letter **A** sound?

Bb

Directions: Look at the uppercase letter **B** and the lowercase letter **b**. Talk about the different lines used to make each one. Trace the letters and then print each one. Look at the pictures of things that start with the letter **B**. Listen to the sound the letter **B** makes at the beginning of each item pictured.

Look Around! Can you find other things that start with the letter **B** sound?

Cc

Directions: Look at the uppercase letter **C** and the lowercase letter **c**. Talk about the different lines used to make each one. Trace the letters and then print each one. Look at the pictures of things that start with the letter **C**. Listen to the sound the letter **C** makes at the beginning of each item pictured.

C C

C C

C C

C C

Look Around! Can you find other things that start with the letter **C** sound?

Dd

Directions: Look at the uppercase letter **D** and the lowercase letter **d**. Talk about the different lines used to make each one. Trace the letters and then print each one. Look at the pictures of things that start with the letter **D**. Listen to the sound the letter **D** makes at the beginning of each item pictured.

D   D

d   d

D   D

d   d

Look Around! Can you find other things that start with the letter **D** sound?

Ee

Directions: Look at the uppercase letter **E** and the lowercase letter **e**. Talk about the different lines used to make each one. Trace the letters and then print each one. Look at the pictures of things that start with the letter **E**. Listen to the different sounds the letter **E** makes at the beginning of each item pictured.

E

e

E

e

Look Around! Can you find other things that start with the letter **E** sound?

Directions: Look at the uppercase letter **F** and the lowercase letter **f**. Talk about the different lines used to make each one. Trace the letters and then print each one. Look at the pictures of things that start with the letter **F**. Listen to the sound the letter **F** makes at the beginning of each item pictured.

F   F

f   f

F   F

f   f

Look Around! Can you find other things that start with the letter **F** sound?

          ©*Teacher Created Resources*

Gg

Directions: Look at the uppercase letter **G** and the lowercase letter **g**. Talk about the different lines used to make each one. Trace the letters and then print each one. Look at the pictures of things that start with the letter **G**. Listen to the sound the letter **G** makes at the beginning of each item pictured.

G G

g g

G G

g g

Look Around! Can you find other things that start with the letter **G** sound?

Hh

Directions: Look at the uppercase letter **H** and the lowercase letter **h**. Talk about the different lines used to make each one. Trace the letters and then print each one. Look at the pictures of things that start with the letter **H**. Listen to the sound the letter **H** makes at the beginning of each item pictured.

Look Around! Can you find other things that start with the letter **H**?

I i

Directions: Look at the uppercase letter **I** and the lowercase letter **i**. Talk about the different lines used to make each one. Trace the letters and then print each one. Look at the pictures of things that start with the letter **I**. Listen to the different sounds the letter **I** makes at the beginning of each item pictured.

Look Around! Can you find other things that start with the letter **I**?

Directions: Look at the uppercase letter **J** and the lowercase letter **j**. Talk about the different lines used to make each one. Trace the letters and then print each one. Look at the pictures of things that start with the letter **J**. Listen to the sound the letter **J** makes at the beginning of each item pictured.

Look Around! Can you find other things that start with the letter **J** sound?

Kk

Directions: Look at the uppercase letter **K** and the lowercase letter **k**. Talk about the different lines used to make each one. Trace the letters and then print each one. Look at the pictures of things that start with the letter **K**. Listen to the sound the letter **K** makes at the beginning of each item pictured.

K   K

k   k

K   K

k   k

Look Around! Can you find other things that start with the letter **K** sound?

Directions: Look at the uppercase letter **L** and the lowercase letter **l**. Talk about the different lines used to make each one. Trace the letters and then print each one. Look at the pictures of things that start with the letter **L**. Listen to the sound the letter **L** makes at the beginning of each item pictured.

Look Around! Can you find other things that start with the letter **L** sound?

Mm

Directions: Look at the uppercase letter **M** and the lowercase letter **m**. Talk about the different lines used to make each one. Trace the letters and then print each one. Look at the pictures of things that start with the letter **M**. Listen to the sound the letter **M** makes at the beginning of each item pictured.

M M

m m

M M

m m

Look Around! Can you find other things that start with the letter **M** sound?

Directions: Look at the uppercase letter **N** and the lowercase letter **n**. Talk about the different lines used to make each one. Trace the letters and then print each one. Look at the pictures of things that start with the letter **N**. Listen to the sound the letter **N** makes at the beginning of each item pictured.

Look Around! Can you find other things that start with the letter **N** sound?

Oo

Directions: Look at the uppercase letter **O** and the lowercase letter **o**. Talk about the different lines used to make each one. Trace the letters and then print each one. Look at the pictures of things that start with the letter **O**. Listen to the different sounds the letter **O** makes at the beginning of each item pictured.

Look Around! Can you find other things that start with the letter **O** sound?

Directions: Look at the uppercase letter **P** and the lowercase letter **p**. Talk about the different lines used to make each one. Trace the letters and then print each one. Look at the pictures of things that start with the letter **P**. Listen to the sound the letter **P** makes at the beginning of each item pictured.

P   P

p   p

P   P

p   p

Look Around! Can you find other things that start with the letter **P** sound?

Qq

Directions: Look at the uppercase letter **Q** and the lowercase letter **q**. Talk about the different lines used to make each one. Trace the letters and then print each one. Look at the pictures of things that start with the letter **Q**. Listen to the sound the letter **Q** makes at the beginning of each item pictured.

37

Look Around! Can you find other things that start with the letter **Q** sound?

Directions: Look at the uppercase letter **R** and the lowercase letter **r**. Talk about the different lines used to make each one. Trace the letters and then print each one. Look at the pictures of things that start with the letter **R**. Listen to the sound the letter **R** makes at the beginning of each item pictured.

R R

r r

R R

r r

Look Around! Can you find other things that start with the letter **R** sound?

Ss

Directions: Look at the uppercase letter **S** and the lowercase letter **s**. Talk about the different lines used to make each one. Trace the letters and then print each one. Look at the pictures of things that start with the letter **S**. Listen to the sound the letter **S** makes at the beginning of each item pictured.

S   S

s   s

S   S

S   S

Look Around! Can you find other things that start with the letter **S** sound?

Directions: Look at the uppercase letter **T** and the lowercase letter **t**. Talk about the different lines used to make each one. Trace the letters and then print each one. Look at the pictures of things that start with the letter **T**. Listen to the sound the letter **T** makes at the beginning of each item pictured.

Look Around! Can you find other things that start with the letter **T** sound?

Uu

Directions: Look at the uppercase letter **U** and the lowercase letter **u**. Talk about the different lines used to make each one. Trace the letters and then print each one. Look at the pictures of things that start with the letter **U**. Listen to the different sounds the letter **U** makes at the beginning of each item pictured.

Look Around! Can you find other things that start with the letter **U** sound?

Vv

Directions: Look at the uppercase letter **V** and the lowercase letter **v**. Talk about the different lines used to make each one. Trace the letters and then print each one. Look at the pictures of things that start with the letter **V**. Listen to the sound the letter **V** makes at the beginning of each item pictured.

Look Around! Can you find other things that start with the letter **V** sound?

Ww

Directions: Look at the uppercase letter **W** and the lowercase letter **w**. Talk about the different lines used to make each one. Trace the letters and then print each one. Look at the pictures of things that start with the letter **W**. Listen to the sound the letter **W** makes at the beginning of each item pictured.

Look Around! Can you find other things that start with the letter **W** sound?

Directions: Look at the uppercase letter **X** and the lowercase letter **x**. Talk about the different lines used to make each one. Trace the letters and then print each one. Look at the pictures of things that start or end with the letter **X**. Listen to the sound the letter **X** makes at the beginning or end of each item pictured.

Look Around! Can you find other things that start or end with the letter **X** sound?

Yy

Directions: Look at the uppercase letter **Y** and the lowercase letter **y**. Talk about the different lines used to make each one. Trace the letters and then print each one. Look at the pictures of things that start with the letter **Y**. Listen to the sound the letter **Y** makes at the beginning of each item pictured.

Look Around! Can you find other things that start with the letter **Y** sound?

Zz

Directions: Look at the uppercase letter **Z** and the lowercase letter **z**. Talk about the different lines used to make each one. Trace the letters and then print each one. Look at the pictures of things that start with the letter **Z**. Listen to the sound the letter **Z** makes at the beginning of each item pictured.

Look Around! Can you find other things that start with the letter **Z** sound?

Write Your Name!

Directions: Think about the letters in your name. What letter does your name begin with? How many letters are there? What is the last letter of your name? Write your name on the lines below and draw a picture of yourself in the frame.

Look Around! Can you find your name printed somewhere? (*in your jacket, on a sign, on an envelope, etc.*)

A–Z Dot-to-Dot!

Directions: This dot-to-dot uses capital letters. First use your finger to trace the letters of the alphabet in order and then use a pencil to complete the dot-to-dot. Color the picture.

Look Around! The next time you are outside, go for an A to Z walk. Look at street signs, car license plates, and names on buildings. See if you can find every letter of the alphabet in order.

Thinking Skills

Critical thinking is an important skill—one that is essential for success in today's changing world. You can work with your child to think more critically anywhere, anytime, through conversations and a variety of activities. The goal is to get children to *analyze* situations, *infer* from the information they are given, *interpret* the data, and *solve* problems to find solutions. Don't worry. It sounds a lot more complicated than it is—it just takes practice.

Start by asking "What if…" questions instead of questions that have *yes* or *no* answers. This will encourage your child to think of different scenarios. For instance, "What if it was snowing and you went outside in your bathing suit?" Ideally, your conversation could take a variety of turns—from silly to serious. Your child might discuss that it would be too cold and that wearing a bathing suit in the snow was a goofy thing to do, or he or she might say it would be important to go back and change, or that he or she should have looked out the window before going outside. Any of these statements could be expanded upon. The focus could be weather, types of clothes, or planning ahead. All of these statements require critical thought. All require a child to think about a situation, make inferences from what he or she knows, think about a plan, and figure out a solution!

It is important to discuss the different ideas and look at things from different angles. Discussions can be matter of fact, or they can be more creative. The key is to get children to feel comfortable thinking and trying new ideas or approaches. Keep in mind that there can be more than one answer or solution to a problem.

Here is another example: suppose you asked your child which food item did not belong in this grouping—cake, pie, ice-cream cone, hamburger. One child might answer that the hamburger did not belong because the other three are desserts. But what if a child said that the ice-cream cone did not belong because it was pointy and the other three foods are round. He or she would not be wrong but had simply looked at it from a different viewpoint. In sharing your two responses to the question, you expand your child's ideas on how to view the world.

Getting Started

In this section, you will find visual prompts (pictures to review), questions to think about and discuss, and problems to solve. It is important to encourage your child to think, and not to rush too quickly give what he or she thinks is the only "right" answer. Encourage your child to answer in complete sentences and to be as descriptive as possible. Try to spend time on each page, and expand on the answers.

Skills to Practice

- Observe closely—What is missing? What is the same or different? etc.
- Consider and discuss different options, approaches, or responses.
- Listen attentively.
- Speak in complete sentences.

Same and Different

Directions: Look at the three items in each row. What are some things that are the same about all three items? Circle the two items that are exactly the same. Point out some differences about the item you did not circle.

Look Around! Stand together in front of a mirror. Take turns naming things that are the same and different about the two of you. (*height, hair length or color, eyes, clothing, etc.*)

Which Two Things . . . ?

Directions: Look at the items in each row. In the first row, color two items that are **hard**. In the second row, color two items that are **soft**. In the third row, color two items that are **round**. Explain your choices each time.

Look Around! How many things can you name that come in pairs? (*shoes, bookends, salt and pepper shakers, etc.*)

Which Three Things . . . ?

Directions: Look at the food items in each row. Cross out the item that does not belong. Explain your reasons. Color the three items that go together the best.

  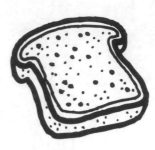

Look Around! Name three things that turn. (*wheels, faucets, doorknobs, steering wheels, etc.*)

What Goes Together?

1

2

3

Look Around! How many articles of winter or summer clothing can you name?
(*jackets, sweaters, scarves, gloves, hats, bathing suits, flip flops, etc.*)

In and On

Directions: It looks like the animals are having fun, doesn't it? Let's talk about the picture of the mouse and the fox and use the words *in* and *on* to describe where things are.

Then you can color the picture.

- What is *on* the fox's back?
- What is *on* the fox's feet?
- What is *in* the mouse's paw?
- What is *in* the fox's mouth?

Look Around! Use a hula hoop or draw a circle on the ground with chalk. Take turns standing *in* the circle and then stepping *on* the circle. Stand *near* the circle and then *far* from the circle.

On and Under

Directions: Look at the picture of the table. What is *on* the table? What is *under* the table? Draw a cup on the table. Draw a ball under the table.

Look Around! Find things in the house that are *on* or *under*. Go outside and look around. Is there something *on* the roof, or *under* a tree?

Up and Down

Directions: Color the bear cub that is *up* in the tree black. Color the bear cub that is *down* on the ground brown. Draw the sun *up* in the sky. Draw a leaf *down* on the ground. Finish coloring the picture.

Look Around! What do you see when you look *up*? What do you see when you look *down*? Look *up* and *down* when you go outside, too!

What Do You Think? Stories

Look Around! Choose a pet, a doll, or a stuffed animal. Imagine an adventure it could go on and tell the story.

Tell the Story, 1, 2, 3

Directions: Look at the three pictures. They are not in order. Explain what is happening in each scene. Write 1, 2, and 3 in the boxes to show the order you think the story goes in and then tell the story.

Look Around! If you see puddles on the sidewalk when you go outside, what do you think could have happened? (*it rained, the sprinklers were on earlier, someone left the hose on, etc.*)

Put It in Order

Directions: Look at the four pictures. They are not in order. What do you think happens first, second, third and last? Write 1, 2, 3, and 4 in the boxes to show the order in which you think the cake was made.

Look Around! Tell a story in three parts. (*First…, then…, and finally (last)…The End!*)

Numbers 1–10

Math is part of everyday life. The activities in this book will help focus students' understanding of a variety of math concepts. The worksheets provide practice writing numbers, connecting numbers to the amounts they represent, counting, sorting, and classifying. Basic shapes are also introduced. Your child can identify, draw, and compare these shapes, looking for similarities and differences.

The activities suggested in the *Look Around!* section at the bottom of each page will help expand children's understanding of math and how it relates to their daily lives.

Getting Started

In this section, your child will be introduced to the numbers 1 through 10. He or she will practice writing the numbers and counting items to represent those numbers. It is important for children to understand "how many" each number represents. Later, focus is placed on sizes, shapes, and on comparing amounts—*more*, *less*, and *equal*.

1 2 3 4 5 6 7 8 9 10

Skills to Practice

- Recognize numbers to 10.

- Count up to 10 objects using one-to-one correspondence—matching number names to the number of objects being counted.

- Name basic geometric shapes.

- Draw common shapes.

- Make comparisons using the terms *same* and *different*.

- Understand concepts of *more than*, *less than*, and *equal*.

- Use positional words to describe relationships among objects.

- Sort and classify to describe relationships among objects.

- Demonstrate a beginning understanding of measurement.

- Begin to recognize and extend patterns.

I Giraffe

Directions: There is one giraffe on this page. Count the giraffe and color it.

Directions: Trace the number **I** with your finger. Then trace and write the number **I**. Start at the arrow at the top and go top to bottom.

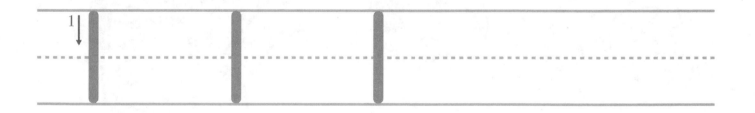

Look Around! Can you find one book? Can you find one table? Go outside. Can you find one blue car?

I Is How Many?

Directions: Look at the groups of toys. Circle your favorite one in each group of toys.

Look Around! Can you find one thing with your name on it? Look in the mirror. What is something on your face you only have one of? (*mouth, nose, chin, etc.*)

62

2 Seahorses

Directions: There are two seahorses on this page. Count the seahorses and color them.

Directions: Trace the number **2** with your finger. Then trace and write the number 2. Start at the arrow at the top, curve around, and make a straight line at the bottom.

Look Around! Can you find two things that are purple? Can you see two tall trees?

2 Is How Many?

Directions: Circle two dogs in each box. Color your two favorite dogs on the page.

3 Mice

Directions: Look at the three mice on this page. Count the mice and color them.

Directions: Trace the number **3** with your finger. Then trace and write the number **3**. Start at the arrow at the top, curve around, and curve around again.

Look Around! Can you find three things that are orange? Name the three orange items you found.

3 Is How Many?

Directions: Tricycles are bikes with three wheels. Circle a group of three tricycles in each box.

Look Around! Can you find a stool with three legs? An easel or a tripod? Read some stories about animals that come in threes? (*Three Little Pigs*, *The Three Bears*, *Three Blind Mice*, etc.)

Triangles

Directions: Look at the triangles below. A triangle is a shape with three sides and three corners. Trace the sides and color the triangles.

Look Around! Can you find triangles in your house or neighborhood? (*signs, fence patterns, tiles, etc.*)

 #8003 1-2-3 Learn

4 Dolphins

Directions: There are four dolphins on this page. Count the dolphins and color them.

Directions: Trace the number **4** with your finger. It has two separate lines that cross in the middle of the long vertical line. Then trace and write the number **4**. Start at the top and draw a line halfway down and cross over to the right. Then make a straight line from top to bottom.

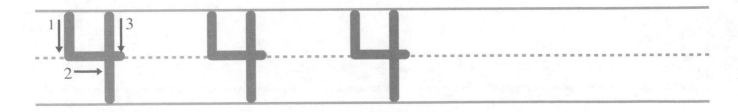

Look Around! Can you find four things that are yellow? Name the four yellow items you found.

4 Is How Many?

Directions: Circle four horses in each corral. Color the horse you would like to ride.

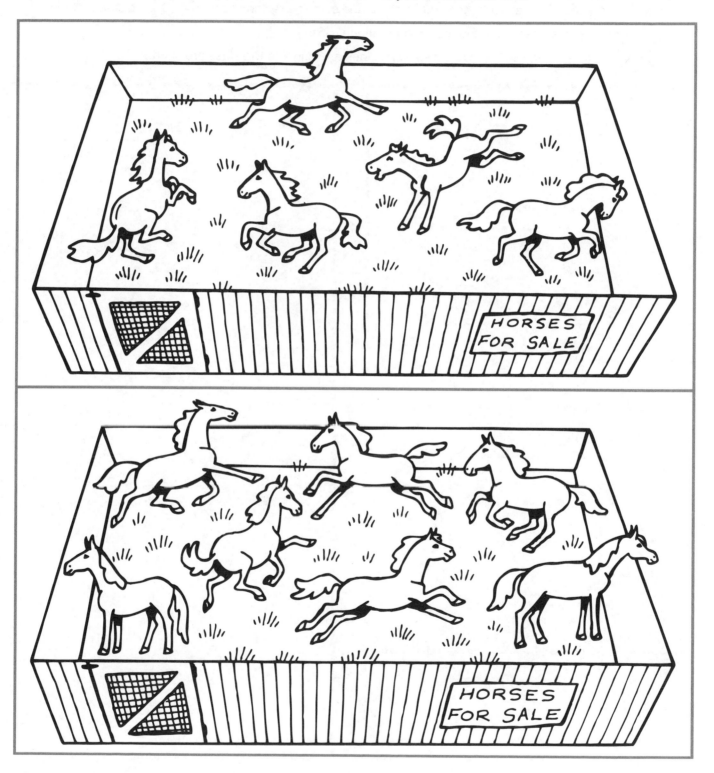

HORSES
FOR SALE

HORSES
FOR SALE

Look Around! Can you find other things with four legs? (*pets, tables, chairs, etc.*)

Squares and Rectangles

Directions: Look at the different shapes below. Compare them. What kinds of lines are used to make them? Trace the sides of the shapes. Color the squares blue and color the rectangles yellow. Draw pictures inside.

A *square* is a shape with four equal sides and four corners.

A *rectangle* also has four sides. Two sides are long and two sides are short.

Look Around! Can you find squares and rectangles in your house or neighborhood? (*windows, doors, tables, etc.*)

5 Starfish

Directions: There are five starfish on this page. Count the starfish and color them. Did you notice that each starfish has five arms?

Directions: Trace the number **5** with your finger. Then trace and write the number **5**. It has two separate lines, like the number **4**. Start at the top, go down halfway and curve around. Then, go back to the top and draw a line —like "putting a hat" on the **5**.

Look Around! Can you find five things that are green? Name the five green items you found.

5 Is How Many?

Directions: Look at each group of objects. Circle five of each object.

5 Fingers

Directions: Trace your child's hand in the center of the frame. Ask him or her to color each finger a different color and then count the fingers.

Look Around! What other parts of your body have five things? (*fingers on each hand and toes on each foot*) Count the fives!

How Many Nuts?

Directions: Look at the squirrels on the page. Each one has a sack of nuts. Count the nuts and draw a line from the nuts to the correct number.

2

4

5

3

Look Around! Can you make groups of 1, 2, 3, 4, and 5? Use nuts, pebbles, or small toys.

6 Animals on Parade

Directions: Look at the six different animals on parade. Count the animals and color them.

Directions: Trace the number **6** with your finger. Then trace and write the number **6**. Start at the arrow at the top and curve around (towards the middle) to make a circle on the bottom.

Look Around! Can you find six things that are white? Name the six white items you found.

6 Is How Many?

Directions: Look at the shapes in each row. Add more shapes to make six shapes in each row.

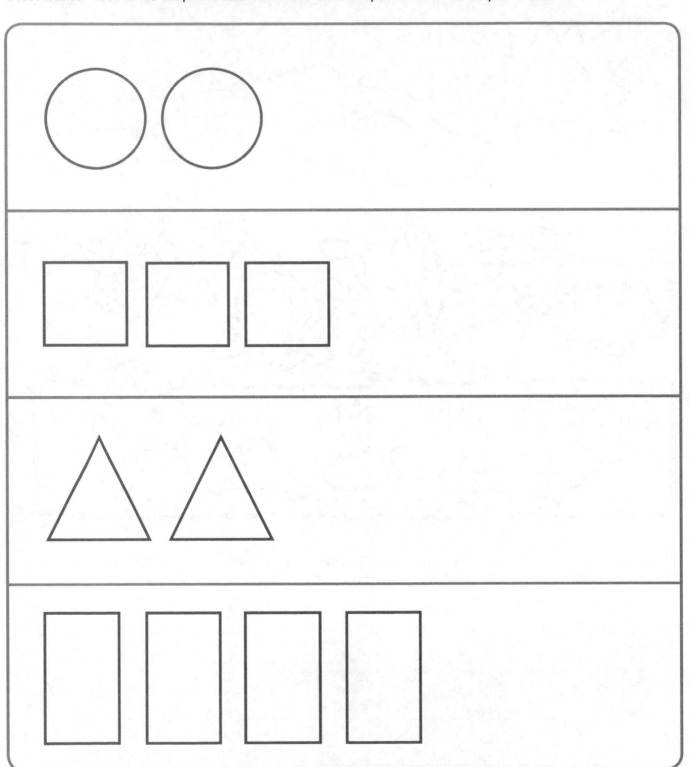

7 Balloons

Directions: There are seven balloons on this page. Count the balloons and color each one a different color.

Directions: Trace the number **7** with your finger. Then trace and write the number **7**. Start at the arrow at the top, move to the right and then make a diagonal line down, aiming back toward the left.

Look Around! Can you find seven things that are red? Name the seven red items you found.

7 Is How Many?

Directions: Look at the picture. Trace the five triangle trees. Add more triangle trees to make seven trees.

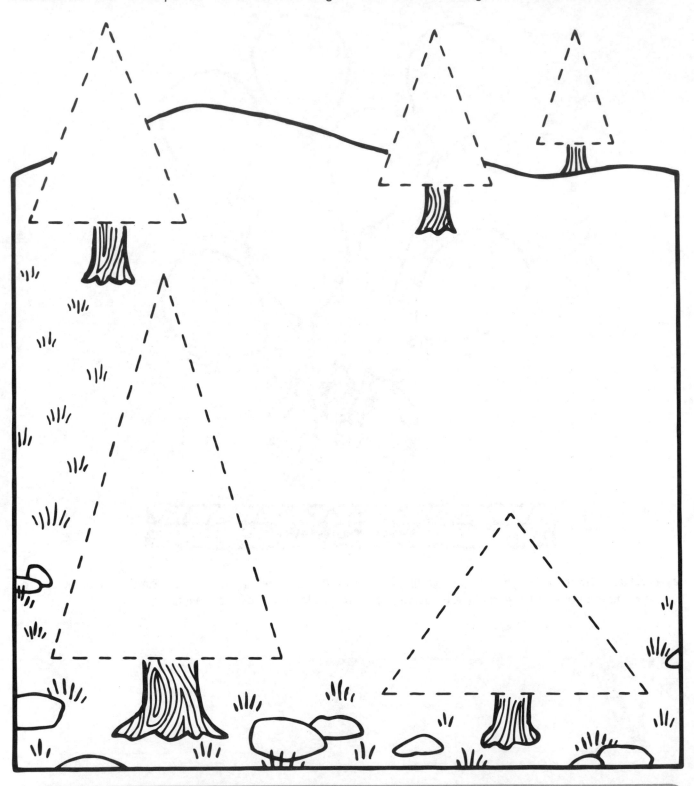

Look Around! Make piles of seven objects or pieces of snack cereal. When you go outside, see if you can find seven trees shaped like triangles.

8 Octopuses

Directions: There are eight octopuses on this page. Each octopus has eight legs. Count the octopuses and color them.

Directions: Trace the number **8** with your finger. Then trace and write the number **8**. Start at the arrow at the top, curve around, cross the midline, and curve around again in the opposite direction.

Look Around! Can you find eight things that are blue? Name the eight blue items you found.

8 Is How Many?

Look Around! The next time you go for a walk, look at the address numbers on houses and license plate numbers on cars. Can you find eight 8s?

9 Snails

Directions: There are nine snails in this garden. Count the snails and color them.

Directions: Trace the number **9** with your finger. Then trace and write the number **9**. Start at the arrow at the top, curve around, make a circle and then draw a straight line down to the bottom line.

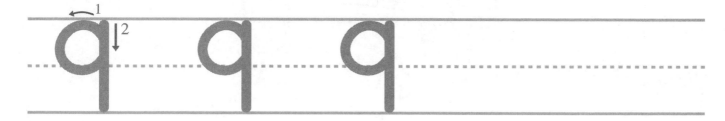

Look Around! Can you find nine things that are black? Name the nine black items you found.

9 Is How Many?

Directions: Look at the hive. There are three bees near the hive. Keep drawing bees until there are nine bees flying around the hive. How many more bees did you need to make nine?

Look Around! Can you line up nine toys or blocks? When you go outside, try to find nine interesting pebbles, shells, or leaves.

10 Frogs

Directions: There are 10 frogs playing at the pond. Count the frogs and color them green.

Directions: Trace the number **10** with your finger. Then trace and write the number **10**. This number is made with a one and a zero. To make the one, start at the arrow and draw a line straight down to the bottom line. A zero is an oval. Start at the arrow, curve to the left all the way to the bottom line, and keep curving back up to the top.

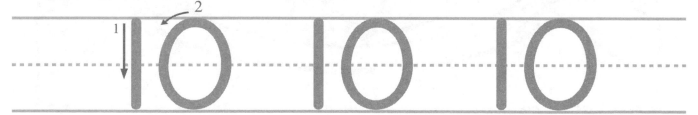

Look Around! Can you find **10** things that are brown? Name the **10** brown items you found.

10 Is How Many?

Directions: Look at all the fish. Color the fish your favorite colors. How many fish are in the fishbowl?

Look Around! Can you count **10** windows in your house? Can you find **10** flowers outside?

#8003 1-2-3 Learn   84   ©Teacher Created Resources

How Many?

Directions: Look at the muffins on each long tray. Circle the correct number of muffins on each tray.

2   4   3

4   5   6

7   8   5

Look Around! Find groups of things to count. (*fruit in a bowl, flowers, towels, etc.*)

Find the Number

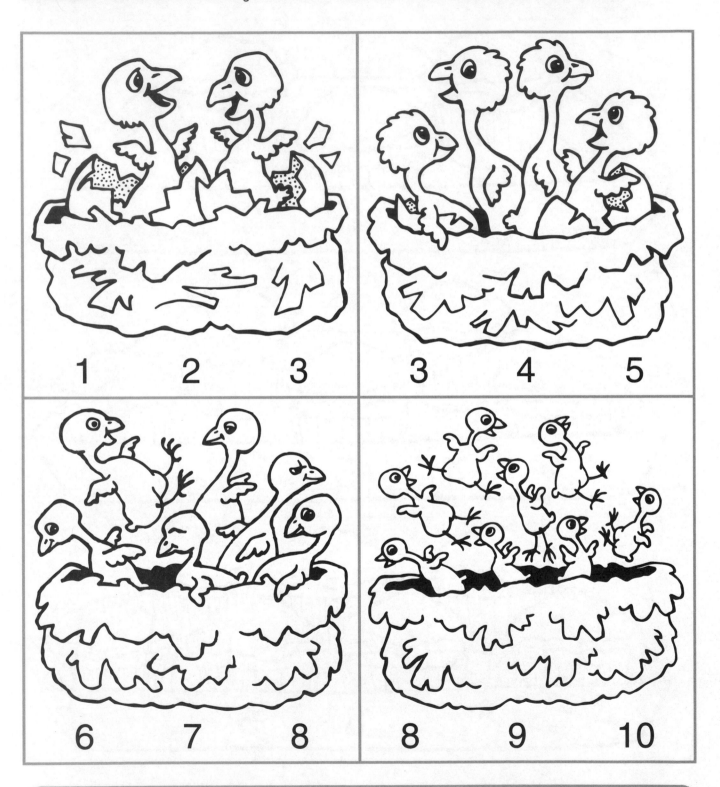

Look Around! At mealtime, count the number of plates, bowls, and forks on the table. What else can you count?

86

Tall and Short

Directions: Look at the people. Two are tall and two are short. Color the shirts of the taller people red. Color the shirts of the shorter people blue.

Look Around! What is the tallest thing you can see? Can you find something smaller than you? What is it?

Large or Small

Look Around! Can you find a large toy and a small toy? When you go outside, look for a large car and a small car. What else do you see that is large or small?

Shapes We Know

Directions: We have observed circles, triangles, squares, and rectangles. Draw a line to match these shapes.

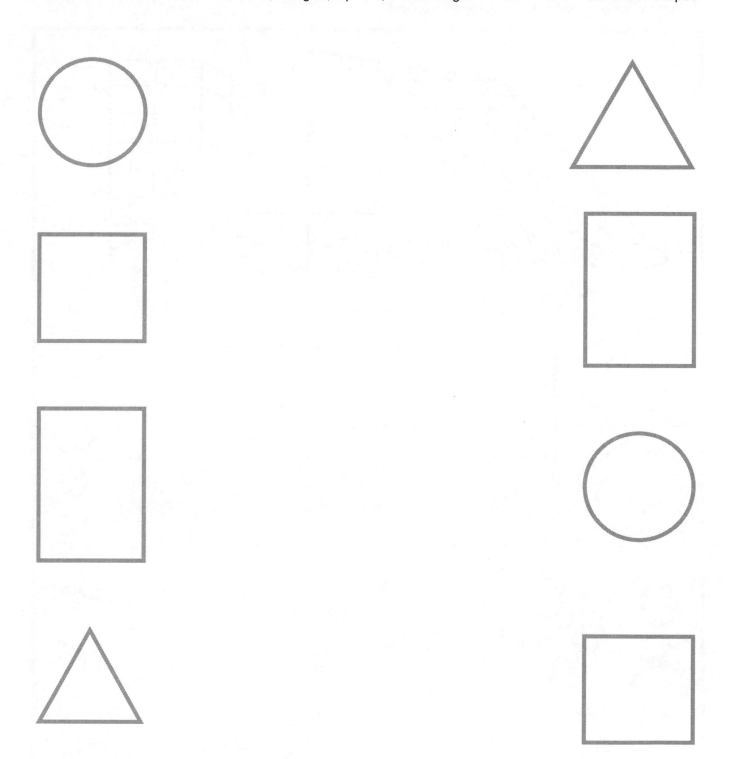

Look Around! When you go outside, look for shapes. Do the same thing in your room. What did you find?

A Shape House

Directions: Look at the lines used to make the picture of the house. Trace the dashed lines to finish the house and color it. How many different shapes can you find?

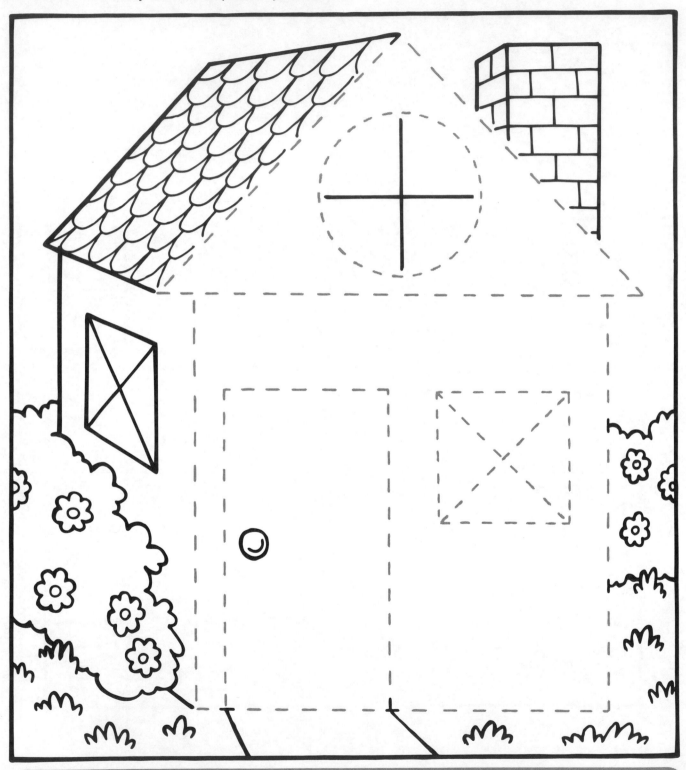

Look Around! What kinds of lines are on your home?

Snowmen

Directions: Look at the different curved lines used to make the snowmen. Trace the curved dashed lines to finish the snowmen scene and color it.

Look Around! What shapes are the tables in your house?

Ovals

Directions: An oval is a curved shape. It looks a bit like a circle but is thinner in the middle—an egg is a good example. Trace the ovals with your finger. Then draw two more ovals on the page.

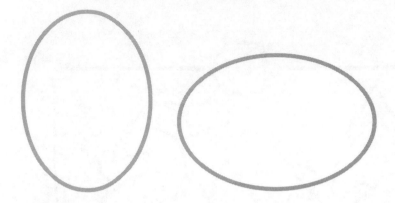

Directions: Imagine the ovals in the basket are Easter eggs. Use crayons to decorate each egg.

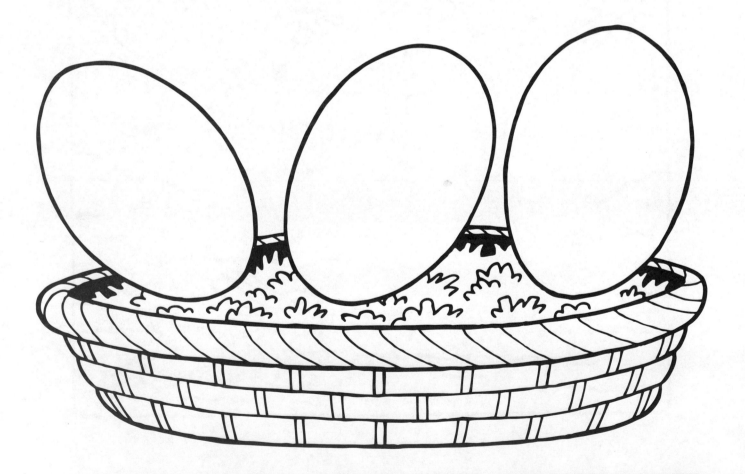

Look Around! Can you find some ovals? Try looking at flower petals, leaves, lights, or dishes.

Rhombus

Directions: A rhombus has four sides formed by straight lines. It is often called a diamond. Trace each rhombus with your finger. Then draw one more rhombus. Try to make each line as straight as you can.

Directions: Use two colors to make a pattern with the rhombuses below.

Look Around! Do you see a rhombus? Do you see a pattern somewhere that uses the rhombus shape?

Trace the Shapes

Directions: The quilt below has many shapes. Follow the Color Shape Key to color each shape. It helps to color the shapes in the key first. Try it! The background can be white, or a color you have not used.

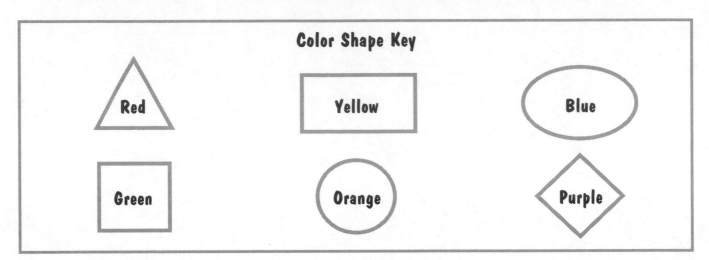

Color Shape Key

Red

Yellow

Blue

Green

Orange

Purple

Look Around! How many different shape designs can you find?

Shape Patterns

Directions: Look at each row. Say the name of each shape out loud. Figure out the shape pattern and then add the next shape. Some patterns can have two shapes and then repeat. Other patterns can have three shapes and then repeat. Color the shapes to keep the pattern.

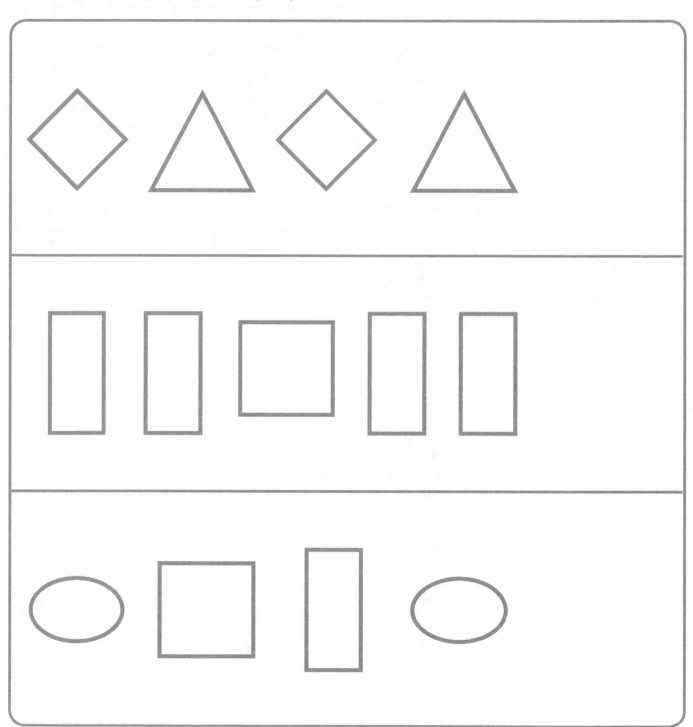

Look Around! Patterns are everywhere. You can even make your own patterns. Try clapping your hands quickly three times and then slowly three times. Repeat it. That is a pattern! Can you think of a different clapping pattern?

What Comes Next?

Directions: We have learned to count to 10. We know that numbers go in a certain order and that each number stands for a certain amount. Let us look at these numbers and write the number that comes next.

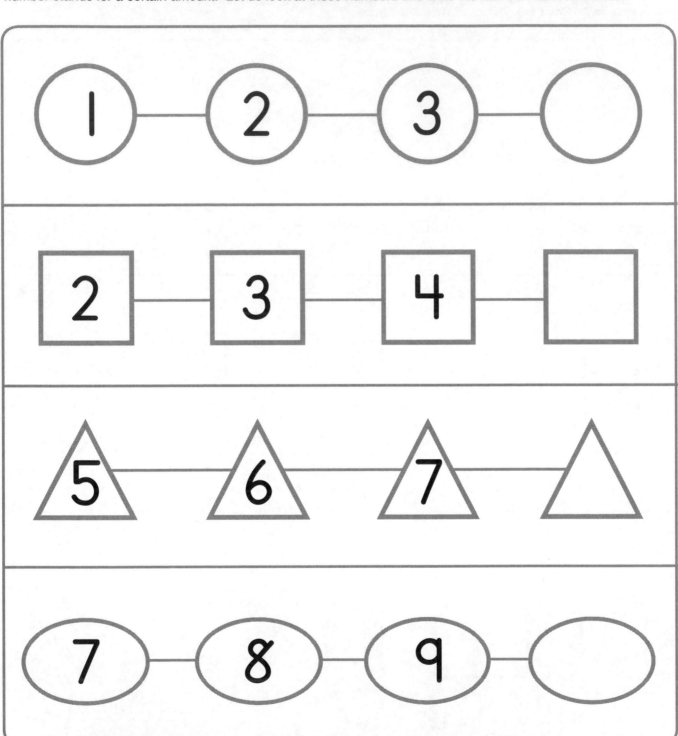

Look Around! Can you make some patterns of your own? Use toy cars, beads, or blocks. (Here are two examples: red bead, blue bead, green bead, red bead, blue bead, green bead, or try one red block, two blue blocks, three yellow blocks....)

Which Group Has More?

Directions: There are two groups of fruit in each box. Count the pieces of fruit in each group. Color the group that has more. Cross out the group that has fewer pieces of fruit.

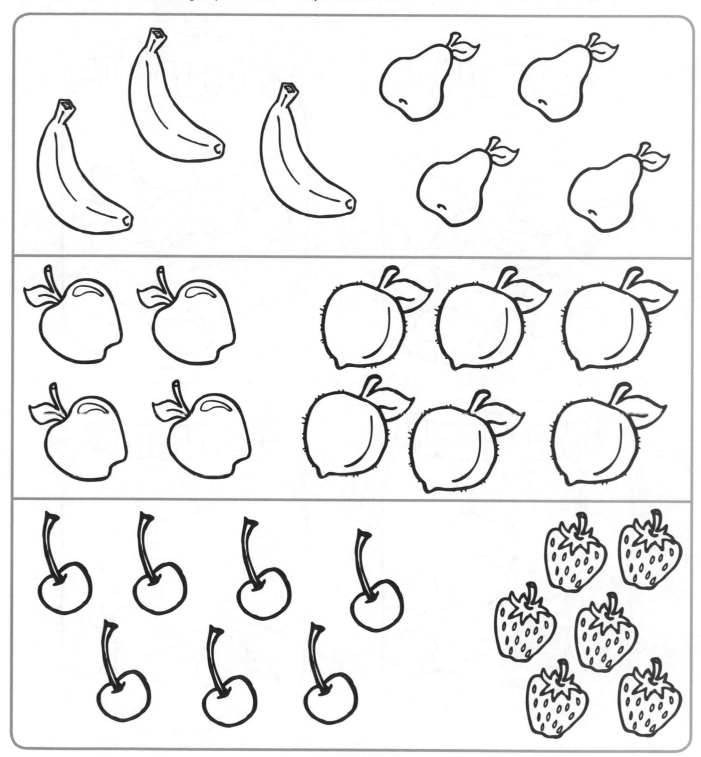

Look Around! Are there more black cars on your street or more white cars?

Which Jar Has More?

Directions: There are two jars in each row. Look at the beans in the jars. Circle the jar that has more beans in each row. Cross out the jar that has fewer beans in each row.

Look Around! Count the tables and chairs in a room. Are there more tables or more chairs?

Equal

Directions: *Equal* means the same amount. Look at the cakes in the column on the left. Draw a line to the cakes with an equal number of candles in the column on the right.

Look Around! The next time you have crackers or grapes or another small snack food, see how many equal piles you can make. Try piles of 2, 3, or 4. When you go outside, see if you have an equal number of windows on each side of the door of the building you live in.

Science and Nature

Science comes naturally to young children as they use their five senses to learn more about their world. They are curious, and their surroundings provide many interesting opportunities to make connections. They are learning names, functions, and uses for many things new to them. Nature is often the starting point—animals and insects, trees and plants, and weather and seasonal changes are all topics that are interesting to observe at an early age.

Getting Started

Focus on the questions your child asks to determine where his or her interests lie and then build upon them. The following activity pages cover a wide range of topics to help you start exploring with your child. Encourage your child to examine the pictures, to think about his or her responses, and to try to answer in complete sentences. (*Example:* How many legs does the spotted cow have? The spotted cow has four legs.) This will help build your child's observation skills and his or her ability to describe things in detail—both very important academic skills.

Skills to Practice

- Make comparisons among objects that have been observed—identify similarities and differences.

- Understand basic concepts related to number, size, color, and shape when observing and comparing.

- Show interest in features of animals that make them unique (*number of legs, habitats, fur or feathers, foods eaten, etc.*).

- Understand how living things function, adapt, and change.

- Use the five senses to explore and observe materials.

- Name major body parts and discuss functions.

- Describe basic needs of living things, such as air and water.

- Differentiate between seasons.

- Understand why different clothing is worn during different seasons.

Make Connections

Use the suggestions given in the **Look Around!** section at the bottom of each page to extend the learning and to make connections between the skill or concept on the page and your child's world.

How Many Legs?

Directions: Look at the different animals in this farm scene. Name each one and count how many legs it has. Color the animals that have four legs. Circle the animals that have two legs. Draw a square around the animal that has no legs.

Look Around! Count the legs on the animals you see. What other differences do you notice? (*fur/hair, feathers, types of teeth, size, colors, etc.*)

Forest or Ocean?

Look Around! Do you live near water, a forest, the desert, or the mountains? What kinds of animals live near you?

Where Does It Live?

Directions: Pets are not wild animals. They can live with us and we need to take care of them. Can you draw a line from each pet to something it might need at your home?

Look Around! Do you have pets? If so, where do they find shelter? Can you find animal homes when you walk around outside? If so, talk about them. How are they made? Are they camouflaged?

Animal Families

Directions: Baby farm animals may look like their parents, but each family member has a different name. Let's learn some of these names and match each baby to its parent. Draw a line from the baby animal to its parent.

calf

pig

chick

hen

foal

ewe

lamb

mare

piglet

cow

Look Around! If you don't live on or near a farm, find books about farm animals or research online. Learn more about these animals and other farm animals.

Living Things

Directions: Plants and animals are living things. They need clean air, food, water, and sun to grow. Circle the things in each row that are living things.

Look Around! Are there new plants or flowers growing near you? Check them every few days and observe how they grow. Discuss the changes.

Plants

Directions: Plants are living things. Most need air, water, sun, and soil to grow. Some plants give us fruit, and others give us vegetables. Others have beautiful flowers. Color the pictures below of things that come from plants. Cross out the things that are not living.

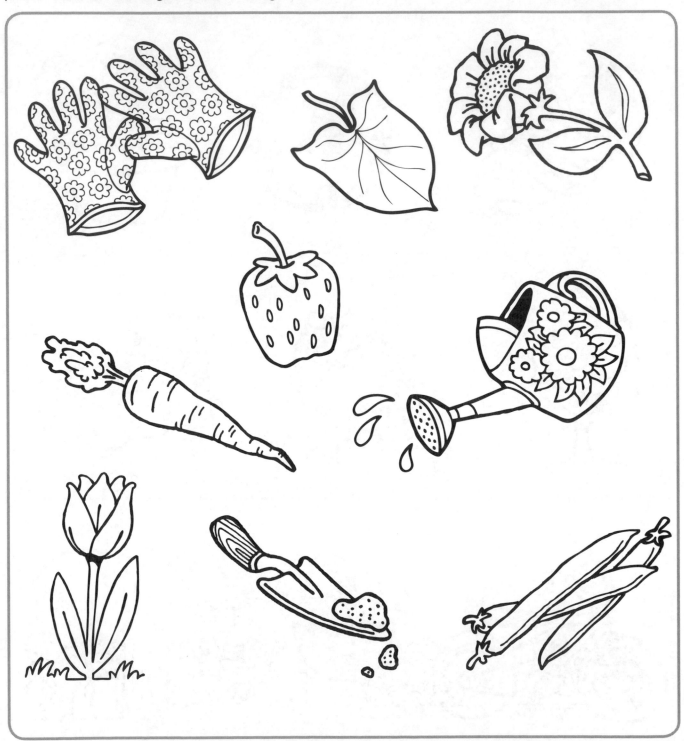

Look Around! Are there plants in your home? Go for a walk and notice how many kinds of plants you can see. Talk about what the plants provide. (*food, beauty, shade, etc.*)

My Body

Directions: Our bodies are pretty amazing. There are many different parts and each does something special. For instance, your neck holds up your head and lets you turn it.

The body parts on this page are like *hinges* that connect two different body parts and help us bend. Point to each picture and name the body part. Circle the picture at the bottom of each box that shows something this body part allows you to do.

Look Around! Can you find some hinges? Look on doors and cabinets.

©*Teacher Created Resources*   107   *#8003 1-2-3 Learn*

Teeth

Directions: Teeth are very important. We need them to talk and to eat. Look at the teeth below and count the teeth on the top and the teeth on the bottom. How many teeth can you count? Color the mouth and teeth.

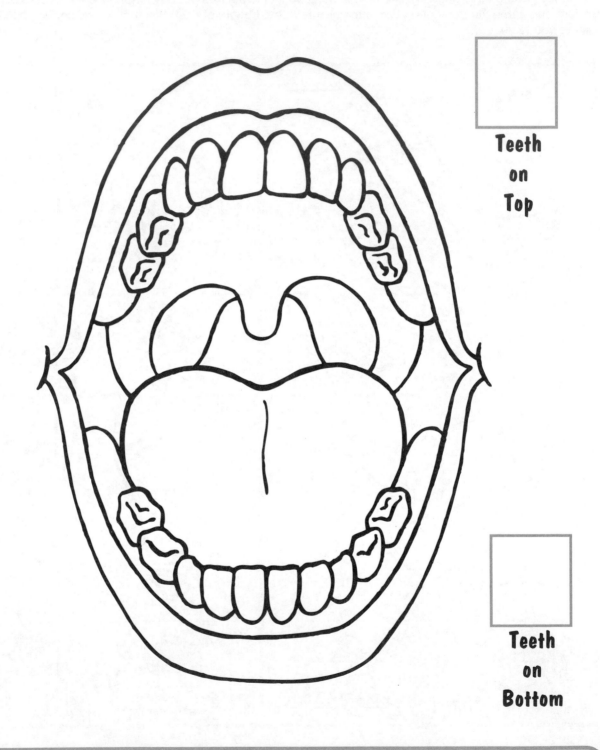

Teeth
on
Top

Teeth
on
Bottom

Look Around! Take a few minutes to look at your own teeth in the mirror. Are they all the same? Which ones do you think are for biting (*front*) and which ones are for chewing (*back*)? Do you have more teeth than the picture, less teeth, or the same amount?

Five Senses

Directions: We have five senses—*sight*, *hearing*, *touch*, *taste*, and *smell*. Let us look at the pictures on the left. They represent each of our five senses. Match each "sense" to a picture of someone using that sense.

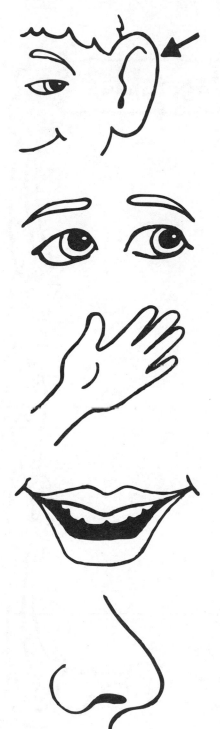

Look Around! Take a Senses Walk. First, what do you *see*? Next, stop for a minute and close your eyes. What do you *hear*? Next, can you find something smooth to *touch*? How does it *feel*? Next, what do you *smell*? Finally, *taste* something when you get back home. Is it salty or sweet?

Healthy Foods

Directions: We know it is important to eat fruits and vegetables every day. Draw pictures of your favorite fruits and your favorite vegetables in the frames below.

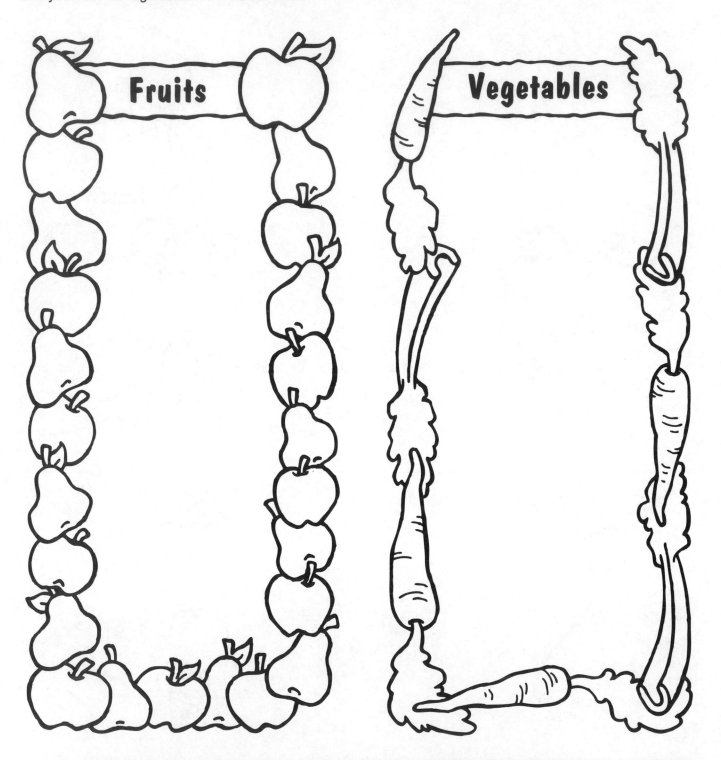

Fruits

Vegetables

Look Around! How many fruits and vegetables can you find in the kitchen? The next time you go to the store or farmers' market, point out five of your favorite fruits and five of your favorite vegetables.

Healthy Foods or Treats

Directions: Every day we try to eat healthy foods for breakfast, lunch, and dinner. This helps us to grow strong and protects us from getting sick. Sometimes, we get to have a treat. Treats are "sometimes" foods. Look at the foods below. Color your favorite foods. Circle the treats.

Look Around! See if you can find four healthy foods and two treats in your house. Look for healthy foods and treats in the grocery store, too.

Directions: Fall is a season when animals like squirrels begin storing nuts for the colder winter months. Leaves begin to change color and fall from the trees. Look at the scene below and point to the signs of fall. Color the picture. Use fall colors to color the leaves. Draw some acorns on the ground for the squirrels. Add a sun.

Look Around! Is it fall where you live? What signs of fall might you see? (*leaves falling, piles of leaves, acorns on ground, people wearing warmer clothes*) Have you ever seen a squirrel carrying nuts? What do you like to do in fall?

Seasons—Winter

Directions: Winter is a season that can be very cold. In some places it snows. In the winter, it gets dark earlier. Birds like geese and robins fly to warmer places. Many bears hibernate. Look at the picture below. How do you know it is winter? Color the picture.

Look Around! Is it winter where you live? What signs of winter might you see? Does it snow where you live? What do you like to do in winter? Have you seen birds flying south?

Seasons—Spring

Directions: Spring is a season when flowers bloom and baby animals are born. It is warmer. We can plant vegetable gardens when the ground gets warm. Look at the picture and name some of the signs of spring you see. Color the picture.

Look Around! Is it spring where you live? What signs of spring might you see in your neighborhood? What do you like to do in spring?

Seasons—Summer

Directions: Summer is usually the warmest season. We can have wonderful gardens, play at the beach, and spend more time outside because the days are longer. Look at the picture below and name some of the signs of summer you see. Color the picture.

Look Around! Is it summer where you live? What signs of summer might you see? What is your favorite thing to do in the summertime?

Social Studies

Social Studies includes the study of people, places, and the environment. In this section, you and your child will be focusing on your family and different types of homes and neighborhoods. You will discuss community helpers and their responsibilities, as well as types of transportation. Finally, you will explore ways to be responsible citizens through recycling and various methods of conservation.

Getting Started

Start with what you know best—your own family! Extend this exploration to different types of homes and the function of different rooms. Move out into the neighborhood and observe different types of buildings, community areas, and land and water features. Learn ways to recycle and conserve natural resources.

Skills to Practice

- Explore the idea of family.

- Compare different types of homes.

- Gather information about your neighborhood and surrounding areas.

- Observe community helpers and other workers.

- Care for Earth through conservation and recycling.

My Family

Directions: There are many kinds of families—young, old, large, and small. Draw a picture of your family in the frame. Circle the number of family members in your picture.

1 2 3 4 5 6 7 8 people are in my family.

Look Around! Look at the families you see at the park or in a restaurant, and count the members. Can you find families that are the same as yours? Can you find families that are different?

Homes

Directions: There are many kinds of homes. Homes provide shelter for us. They keep us warm and safe. Look at the homes below. Color the one that is most like yours. Is it an apartment, a house, a houseboat, or a mobile home? Circle the one you would like to live in someday and explain why.

Look Around! If you could live in one of the three little pigs' homes, would you want the one made of straw, sticks, or bricks? Explain your choice.

The Rooms in a Home

Directions: There are different rooms in homes, and we do different things in each one. Look at the rooms below. Draw a line to an item that would go in each room.

Look Around! What is your favorite room in your home? Why? If you could design a special room, what would be in it?

The Neighborhood

Directions: There are many different kinds of neighborhoods. They can be in the city or the country. Some are filled with houses or apartments. Others have very tall buildings. Some have parks, stores, and other important buildings. Talk about the buildings shown below. Then match the places below with items you might find in a neighborhood.

Look Around! Explore your neighborhood and see which buildings you can find. Are there other special buildings in your neighborhood?

Community Helpers

Directions: Community helpers are people who help us. Look at the pictures below and discuss each community helper's job. Then draw a line to the object that worker might use.

Look Around! Do you know any community helpers? If so, what do they do? If not, which one would you like to meet?

Jobs People Do

Directions: Look at the pictures below and discuss each person's job. Then draw a line to the object that worker might use.

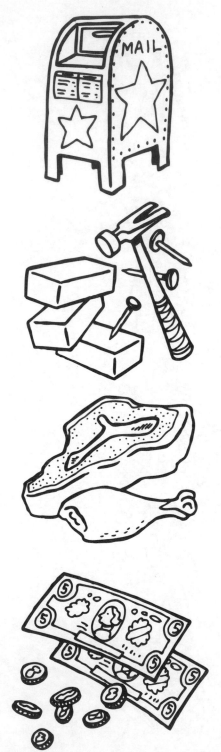

Look Around! What jobs do your parents do and what tools do they use? The next time you are helping run errands, notice the jobs people do in each place that you go. Is that a job you would like to have? Why or why not?

Land, Sea, or Air

Directions: We see many types of transportation each day. Some vehicles have wheels and travel on roads, some have wings and fly in the sky, and still others can float and move on water. Let's think of some other vehicles that could be in the sky, on the water, or on the road. Add another vehicle in the sky. Color the picture.

Look Around! What kinds of transportation have you used? The next time you go for a walk or a drive, see how many different vehicles you can find. Don't forget to look up!

Don't Litter

Directions: It is important to take care of where we live. Don't litter. Always throw your trash in a trashcan. We need to help keep our home and neighborhood clean. Work together to answer the questions.

1. How is the boy in the picture taking care of where he lives?

_____

_____

2. What can you do to take care of your neighborhood?

☐ _____

☐ _____

3. Color the picture.

Look Around! Help empty the trash in your home. Remind people not to litter.

Keep the Air Clean

Directions: Cars and other vehicles can cause the air to get dirty. One way to help keep the air cleaner is to walk or ride a bike or scooter when you can instead of driving. The children are walking and riding. They are helping keep the air clean, and they are getting exercise! Work together to make a plan.

1. How can your family help keep the air clean?

     ☐ _____

     ☐ _____

     ☐ _____

2. Color the picture.

Look Around! If you are going somewhere close to your home, try leaving a little earlier and walking or riding instead of going in a car or taking the bus.

Save the Trees

Directions: Trees are very important. They are homes to many animals, and they provide shade when it is hot. We get wood to build things from trees, and paper is made from trees. It is important to save trees when we can. One way to save trees is to use less paper and another is to recycle paper.

1. Think of ways you can save trees. Work together to make a plan.

   ☐ _____

   ☐ _____

   ☐ _____

2. Color the picture below.

Look Around! See how many things in your house are made of paper. (*books, notepads, calendars, newspapers, labels, etc.*)

Save Water

Directions: Clean water is very important and we should not waste it. People, plants, and animals need water to live and grow.

1. What is the child in the picture doing to save water?

   _____

   _____

2. What can you do to save water? Work together to make a plan.

   ☐ _____

   ☐ _____

   ☐ _____

3. Color the picture.

Look Around! Where does water come from? (*faucet, hose, rain, water tower, snow on mountains, lakes, etc.*) See how many water sources you can find in your house and in your neighborhood.

Save Energy

Directions: Electricity is one kind of energy. We can store it and use it to make the lights, the computer, and the television work. Some cars run on electricity, too. Work together to answer the questions below and write down one or two ideas to help save energy.

1. What is the child in the picture doing to save energy? _____

   _____

2. What can you do to save energy?

   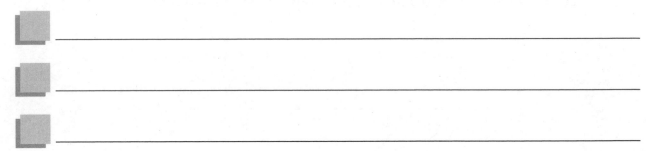

3. Color the picture.

Look Around! What needs electricity in your house? (*lamps, lights, dishwasher, washing machine, computer, etc.*) See how many things you can find in your house and in your neighborhood that run on electricity.